AF405614

Stars Within

A JOURNEY BEGAN IN FINDING MYSELF IN THE DARKNESS

This book is Self-published.

Illustrations by @lakshita, @michelle.

Printed in 2025.

LAKSHITA

To heart,
To each heart out there who loves, hurts, feels and
cherishes.

PROLOGUE

It was a rather unexpected evening for a little girl. The stairs probably marked the beginning of the voyage in this gigantic sea of memories and poetries.

Who would've known walking down the street to see the rainbow would fill colours throughout this first book?

It's been almost 10 years since I've held that pen, and I guess I've burnt more words than written.

At first, I wrote about my friends, what I saw, and what I felt. Then, sadness took over, and I wrote all that I could to escape the misery.

Then someone saved me from all of it, only to shower heavy rainstorms.

But, I didn't let that stop me. The more bad came into my life, the more I wrote.

The best that I've written is when others inspired me: movie actors, fictional characters, random strangers or strangers in my school and college. I delved into their experiences and tried to feel them like my own.

That is mostly what happens when life gets uneventful for a writer.

I have written about the flings that I had and the letdowns. I was never fortunate enough to have a happy and joyous experience with someone to write gleefully about it.

And I have no complaints because then I wouldn't be writing the preface to my first-ever poetry novel. Because I reflected that I was only able to write about the wrongs and the bad that happened in my life as I would just be too lost when happy moments were taking place.

After plenty of research and guidance from my book mentor
Ms. Vijayashanthi Ma'am who teaches English in the college
where I study, I am finally able to see my dream coming true.
I also want to give credit to my parents and my sister for
listening to me read out the poems during dinner and while
they were watching their favourite shows.
Last but not least, I would like to thank the world for
showering upon me such experiences and enabling me to write
about them.

In this book, you'll go through all the different phases that I
went through. It will start with an impulse, a mild breath,
leading you straight into the feelings of a teenage girl—the
feeling of belongingness, fondness, yearning and compassion.
To make it real and believable you will experience the torment
and sorrow one feels after their childhood toy one day goes
missing under the bed.
The end of the book tries to replicate the end of something
bigger, something special which is too grand to be expressed in
words. And the curtain falls.

I hope you relish reading it as much as I bled writing it.

LIFE

Her

She was a girl
With dreams to fulfill
With aims to achieve
But was kept in the dark
By the cruel world
She was tamed and tortured
She was hated by monsters
She screamed for help
She ran for herself
Until she reached the end
Of the road and the world
It was dark and terrifying
She ran until she was paralyzed
She fell on the stones
She wished she was never born
But she was saved
She was protected by a spirit
It took her to a home that was safe
She woke and felt she was born again

Time Travel

I could see the scars on me
The filthy faults in me
When I traveled back
To the younger me

I knew it was alright
Sun doesn't always shine bright
But what to do about these faces
Who made me cry over them the whole night

I've been cheerful all this time
Since I stopped committing that crime
Accepting what others think
And loving me, 'cause I am all mine

And the reason I traveled time
Was to know how I climbed
Every tear, every scream
To know good things takes time

Kalon

I feel like a Kalon
When I'm sleeping beside myself
But see me as a demon
When I look at myself in the mirror
My shadow torments me under the blankets
My breathing sounds like a thunderstorm
The curtains I drew
Fall apart in every ray
The mountains I blew
Come back to me in every way
But my cheeks are softer than ever
As if the clouds listened to my wish
Even though I could not stand, never
But I ran miles, I was fast as a kiss
And now I'm still
Like the lakes, like the sorrow
Like a heart has gone hollow

Is It Dried Up?

Nothing ached more than this red
With green blood all over it's ground
Hiding behind the devil's head
A deserving hand in the crowd
Is missing
And missing again
I went all over the city and back
Looking for it
In someone's hands
Dead in someone's garden
Alive in someone's book

Pace Of Life

These trains are moving so fast
Keeping pace with them is harder than ever
I lit myself a candle at last
Wishing it will give me light forever
Can't hold on to the same winds anymore
They might take me somewhere dark
I hoped I could turn my boat to the shore
So I didn't have to keep up with the mark
But they keep on pushing me
Like it's them who give me strength
They don't know that they just coerced me
And I just measured my journey's length

Just One More

I stapled the pages
One more member on the shelf
Took another paint on my hands
Another scream on the walls
A new scar on my skin
An old hour of trying
Another memory of bliss
Another day of crying
Maybe I'll create a new life
But not the same as mine

Sunny Chaos

The evening chores
With those wild dreams
Have always kept a secret
But it is hard to believe
The sun when shines
It shines so bright
That all the eyes forget their work
And we keep them shut tight
Though the morning is always beautiful
It is meant to be calm
But the sounds of these walking souls
Keep disturbing like an alarm
The bodies, the minds
Are capable of what's beyond
But the heart and the soul
Have the purest bond

Vintage Tale

They got your folktales, they got your jewels
Spinning around the country
In your old Mustang
They threw the flyers, called you a slut
Painting around the walls
The traces of your face
The disguise of your blame
Your skin, too dark; your hair, too short
You're either too tall, or you're a dwarf
Called you names that belonged to no one
They sent out their men, no one could see 'em
The beard and the dirt, the hunger of the skirt
They got your lip shade, they got all your rings
Got all your reasons to build heartstrings
They left you shattered, they left you torn
Your name on the brothel with the spelling wrong
They got hold, you gave in
They got stronger, you got weak
Until someone came for your rescue
Hope that someone isn't you
His name should be hidden, his face unknown
For what he did, he did for you
Saving your life, he somehow saved his own

Life's Own Home (I)

The world went blind
As the sky smiled
On this fateful maid
Of the king's wife
She was robbed of all
Jewels and crowns
Her place was taken
And was torn down

The streams went silent
As the flowers dried
Around the home of the man
Whose young lover died
He waters the plants
Cooks the food
He tries to smile
His mouth barely moves

Life's Own Home (II)

The trees went naked
On the empty farmland
Owned by an orphan
Who has to hold no hand
He irrigates with his tears
Cuts with his small knife
He is on his own
He learns how to survive

And so the universe divine
On his beloved creatures
Gives off a blessing
To the three breathers
And the maid got her jewels
The flowers bloomed again
The child played on the man's lap
And since then they have seen no pain

I

I didn't look up high
I didn't look in his eyes
I was the one
Where my own sky lied
So I didn't look for the moon
I didn't travel to Mars
I didn't wait for something good too soon
I made myself my own star

If I was Better

I wish I had written the way I thought
More decisively
More of me drowning in my own misery
My voice screaming out of betrayal
Hatred running in my veins
My own hands choking my neck
The once-loved flowers, they tell me I'm brave
The white daisies
Oh, the white daisies
How have I loved them all in and out
How I felt safe and noticed by them
Though they are just flowers, look at what they did to
me
To my eyes, to my soul, to my pyrrhic body
And so I wish them to be on my grave
In and out
I'll take them buried within my soul
I'll take them to my imaginary home
I'll gift myself a dying hope

Luscious Green (I)

I kept writing about a sunrise that might mark a new
life
A sun that shines but never gives out fire
On this lush green grass under my feet, I rub my hands
as I say my name
It sounds so unfamiliar and I don't know its taste
But the words call out another miracle out of me
The winds were so calm and cold, brushing against my
face
I kept dreaming of a place that might be destiny
Surrounded by invaders and sceptred by thieves I call
out your name
All I get is the silence so loud that I hear the water
falling down the lane
I wished to climb those mountains someday
But my will doesn't move on itself
And my body remains here, unharmed, immovable
And while I tear down the pages of my diary and burn
them to ashes

Luscious Green (II)

In the fire I built by lightning my heart and yours
In this lush green grass, sitting here with my head tilted
towards the sun
I see the home that I built with the garden I kept and
the books I read
And the waterfall where we first met
I knew it all at once
As I was going up the air
So high that you seem so small to touch me
So far that you seem too weak to hurt me
So distant that you seem like a stranger to see me, who
needs me

Who am I?

I stand in front of the mirror
And just think
I think of who I am
Is it me standing in front of my reflection
Or just another creation of this generation

To my younger Self

And I knew I could do it
I could turn back the things I ruined
I needed to tell myself I love her
And that she had a whole universe inside of her
Her soul was pure but weak
Her heart was sensitive, it used to bleed
I needed to tell my parents
They are everything I could ever ask for
They were my spirit and my home
And without them, I'd be alone
But all I did
Was blamed for it all
To make me who I am, a room with no walls
If only I could do it
I would travel the time
And do everything right

Angel Baby

Can't ever have enough
The inner battles fight this voyage
Constantly diving into unfathomable oceans
Seas of despair
Woods of hope
On the verge of falling
To die or to rise
That's the compromise
It's nothing but a lie
Or is it just
Rewinding all the times
Of sacred joy for sinner crime
Oh, this is absurd
Mon ange it whispered
Breathtakingly worthy
The eyes closed
My will's audacity
To grow vulnerable
My faith's insufferable
My guard unbreakable

Don't Believe Me

Don't ask me about it
My heart said and my mind forgot
Knew no other guilt
My words shouldn't be locked
Though you have the key
The riches are all mine
And I wouldn't let you keep
The moments I disguise
So don't ask me about it
Don't say it all out aloud
Because my heart and mind is
Nothing but two worlds apart

The Search

She walks past the moments
That remind her of her weakness
She holds on to these waves
Not to remember her homesickness
She believes lies are just like flowers
Can be beautiful, or unappealing
Sometimes torn, sometimes healing
But she considers truths to be merely words
That just hit someone like thorns
And bleed reality out of their veins
That was hiding in for long
She crosses her fingers again
Hoping to be lost somewhere
Where no one sees her smile, knows her pain
The place she wanted was rare
She looks and looks and finds
Then one day She reaches back home
Home, where she hid her soul

A Wanderer

A wanderer is what I feel like lately
As I slowly walk those fields
Gasping the fragrant air
To fill my lungs with
Recollection of those dreams
That never dare to come true
I feel like a wanderer
When I see his face in the clouds
A face so unknown but familiar
That vanishes as the moon arrives
At its edge to call up the night
And the night, should I call you my enemy
As you make me feel the need
To have a roof over and a floor beneath
But I, as a wanderer
Will fulfill the word's aspirations
To live like a wanderer
And to die too like one

My Body Protects Me

I listened to my heart saying
It's okay, it's okay, it's okay
I accepted it and kept on praying
I hope this okay forever stays
I knocked at my mind
It said I'm awake and well
That's what I needed at night
So I sleep and dream on a shell
I heard my soul talking to a stranger
It'll be alright, I'm here, trust me
They seemed to be a reminder
The one my heart keeps forgetting
For the last time, my lips talked
They uttered or whispered a word
Wish I could hear it while I walked
I wish I could know my worth

All I Need (I)

All I need is a cup of coffee
To keep me awake this night
To write down my thoughts
And to relive the pasts of my life

All I need is one more content moment
'Cause I lack a smile
And I've to keep it unrevealed from the world
Not like the epoch when I was a child

All I need is some ink for my pen
It has to keep on rolling down the pages
Of the book of my life which is bounded
From going to all the surreal places

All I Need (II)

All I require is the light of the moon
To fall on my face tonight
To let the stars see that I glow just like them
When I unpack my secrets by the light

All I need is just one more drop of tear
As I've been holding on for so long
When control loses, the world wins
But I'm free now as I am where I belong

All I need is some time to recall
What it would be like if I wasn't living like
this
If I was complete and whole
And was not reminiscing about the bliss

Reap and Sow

That pain has been beautiful
At least it is all meaningful

Those tears are worthy
Even though they make my vision blurry

Those sombre days were dignitary
Ecstatic that they filled my library

The clouds were extraordinary
Which shed raindrops on my life diary

That past life surely was regretful
Which gave birth to a new one so fruitful

Unknown

I'll wash my fears away with the pain
To accept the glory of my vein
I shall not defend your desires
Which I'm holding in my breath
I will keep up the pace of the rain
And admire the mighty
Shall not be noticed my agony
Which I accepted with your aspirations

We've Grown

To all the shadows that were spoken
To all the silence that prose
To all the wounded that's risen
To all the scared who's bold
I raise this toast
As we all have grown

For all the times someone smiled
For all the eyes that were left dry
For each time the sun shined
For all the beauty divine
I raise this toast
As we all have grown

As far as I see, the old and the young
And I still can, the view seems fun
And as far as it seems, it still seems close
Something I got, which I longed for
I raise this toast
For we all have grown

LOVE

Right Time, Wrong Person

'Cause when we first met in my backyard
I never knew I could fall so hard
Then you said your name and you took my hand
I was shaking all inside, trying to understand
Is it all for real or were you just a daydream
'Cause the touch was supposed to heal, all my nightmares and
empty screams
But it gave me more
It gave me all the beasts I read in diaries
All extremes add to my anxiety
But was it worth the wait
Of all the years
I spent in the grave
With all hopeless fears
To find you all again
I crossed the boundary lines
But it was the wrong train

You Had Me

You saw me falling from the stars to the flower beds
You saw me dancing on the edge of a river cliff
You saw me counting the leaves on those oak trees
You saw me flying with the birds in the direction of the
breeze
You heard me singing in the woods and whistling in peace
You saw me reading the lines on the walls and those city
streets
You saw me crying on a mountain on those wheat fields
You saw me laughing with the horses and sheep in the June
heat
You saw me looking at you with a beam how you were
looking at me
You saw me falling for you at that very moment I believe
But then you saw me going back from where I came in
mystery
And hence you were glad to ever see me
And how I always knew
That I was being seen by you

Hurt Me Instead

I believe what you said about me
I believe every word of it
The letter didn't just have ink
It had scars engraved on them
That cut through me
As each word touched my lips
As much as it hurts me
I know it hit you harder
Or I wouldn't be reading this
I would be listening to it rather
And I know these scars
Will forever be there
But I wish they were mine
For you, I'd take them

He was a Man (I)

His hands hold
The darkness in me
As he stands close
Marking me his

I read his mind
Every single thought
The pain in his eyes
As the silence drop

He thinks of me
Night and day
So let me repeat
The words he said

"I will die if I must
But you'll live long
I shall turn to dust
Where you may stand strong"

He was a Man (II)

And this was one
Letter he wrote
Didn't mention love
Or hate at all

But I read his mind
And he hid it all
Hate and love alike
He let me fall

He was But a man
Soulless and small
In the back of my hand
Where I cut it all

If Only

Maybe it's too early to say
Or maybe it is just too much
But I think I found my home
With a rainbow roof above
I could not see him
But I could feel his touch
He cares and he's kind
But sometimes makes me mad, sort of
He tells me I'm beautiful
Even when he hasn't seen me
I tell him it's kind of unbelievable
I know I have a future to see
Which I thought I didn't deserve
But you made me feel that I was enough

Be Mine

There will be lightning in my bones
When I'll see you for the first time
There will be silver-gold snow
When I ask you to be mine

I'll let you know

I'll tell you a beautiful lie
Once I'm fully alive
Why my eyes never glow
Why I've never liked snow
This is the question I ask
Even myself in the last
I almost forget everything
But even almost means nothing
As long as I remember
That one night in November
That one touch on my skin
That got me chills from within
And I'll tell you a harsh secret
When I feel the weakest

Child's Love (I)

He did come to me that day
He was still like an ocean lying in peace
He was silent as if the moon was resting
He was just shivering as the rays of the sun
It was quite
Motionless
But in that moment I could hold an eternity
I could see through his eyes to his heart and say
That he was in love
He, who was just a bud in a garden full of flowers
Finally blooming in rainbow colors
He was happy, nervous, excited and joyous
He didn't show anything
He couldn't
He held his breath and looked up at me
His hands which were behind
Now came like a sudden shower
He was holding a flower

Child's Love (II)

That flower was just like him, blooming
But not to say that it was more beautiful than a fully bloomed
one
It was lively
It gave a sense of happiness
A sense of belonging
That was hidden inside for years
He who was blooming shy
Couldn't say those words He wanted to
I too couldn't hold anything inside
So I stood there holding that flower
He and I were still
He and I were silent, but
He and I were in a moment of eternity

I'll Stand By You

Whenever things go wrong
Or you are upset
I'll help you stand strong
I swear on the sunset
I'll stand by you

Whenever you want to cry
And you are feeling exhausted
I'll remain by your side
I swear on the autumn
I'll stand by you

When you know what you want
And you're trying hard to achieve it
I'll make you believe that you'll perceive it
And then I swear on the oceans
I'll stand by you

At a time when you're successful
And happiness lies within you
You'll also love me and be trustful
And I swear on the dew
I'll always stand by you

And I understand your decision
Of repudiating me in helplessness
And now I'll hold my emotions
And again I swear on the sky
I'll always stand by you

You

You became my art
Which is hidden
From you and me
'Cause I never want you to know
And I don't want myself to remember

You Were Neon Green (I)

You said you're not used to it
And I said I understand

I thought I should be more considerate
Given I was braver

You kept saying sorry for something you didn't regret
I said 'It's okay' so you're not upset

So do I keep living like it's nothing
Like all my feelings have died inside me
And what if, if you did try
Someday you might like
Me

Did you even think that?
Before giving me a heartache
But I guess I was dumb enough
to believe the empty words

I know now
Falling for people is not right
You cannot win some fights

You Were Neon Green (II)

So my hollow heart will stay dead
The lifeless in me had lost life again
This time no offense
You were good
But you made me sad
Even though I didn't deserve it
I'll take just what's coming
And sleep tonight
knowing I won't be dreaming
Again

Her &Him

She hates when the world turns up on her
She feels the most miserable than ever when she's around
people who make her feel ashamed of being herself
She misses her home with closed curtains and lights turned
off, so she could sleep soundly in the night without the
moon's light falling up on her eyes and waking her up
She cries out in silence because she knows no one will care
to listen to her screams even if she is loud
She calls out for help, even though she knows no one will
come for her but he
She knew he would come for her and take her from the
cruelty she faces
But neither does she know about him, nor does he think he
is the one

For Everything

For all the times that I knocked on your door
I would keep a rose
For all the times I wrote you letters, unsent
I would lock my door
I could sing every song and never miss a beat
But the one that I miss is you
I could swear on my life, the mistakes I won't repeat
But I can't learn something new
I would keep writing your name on my bedroom wall
For each letter, I'd tear apart
I would keep on wearing the same old shirt you got me
So I could be your forgotten art
And I know that forgiving is a little tricky
I've seen all the ones you used on me
So for each time, I fall out of my sleep
I would keep a rose
And on my wrecked floor with the doors closed
I'd bleed out and it'd be my home

I shall Not

I shall not discourage your will
I shall not give you pain and suffering
I shall not admire you
I shall not surround you with grief
I shall not hold you back
I shall not let you have
Me

Mountains High

I climb to the fields
Where he and I first met
Where every wound heals
And our souls are never upset

I would sleep on the grass there
For as long as life holds me
Wish eternity could be here
To let me stay here and breathe

He returns to me
On the fields
He knew where he was supposed to be
That he's supposed to be with me

Was it 'Us'?

It was the harshest
The kindest
The bustling and finest

The time I spent
Thinking
'us' and 'we' could be timeless

So I wrote a song
To imprison the time
When you and I were
infinite

And you held my gaze
For longer than before
It was an unspoken confess

Words were my way
To express care and pity
They were my abiding
mistress

But when they didn't leave your mouth
As they were supposed to
Maybe then, I was broken by two

One being my mercurial
lover
The other unlikely
My script of defiance

Your Library Is Me

Inside me, it was all you
And outside of me I just don't wanna look
Besides all of my mistakes, there was an I love you
And I was like a romantic incomplete book

Waiting to be finished after being yours forever
Dying to know if it could be us through the shadows
The way that I want to be loved ever
Is on the way whose path is led by the arrows

The moon will hate me for that
To love someone more than it
But I'll still remember the days when I was sad
To let me know that I wouldn't be this happy if I would've quit

But now I don't wanna lie anymore to myself
That how much more will I be living in my dreams
Consoling my soul that it's forever held
And that without your memories I can still scream

Predictions

I knew the ending
But still celebrated the beginning of us
I hated the rhyming
But still sang the song of lust
I kissed the consequences
Of that never-ending thirst
I threw every pen
But still wrote with the blood on my hands
I saw a nightmare
But still lived it like a dream that never ends

I Belong to You

They say home is where you belong
Oh but will I ever find mine
They say home is trust
I never got your trust in time
Or were you so foolish
To make me weak
And leave me here rotten
Oh you were a monster
Who broke my heart
And left my soul open
Did you never see the love
Did you never see the faith
I kept you close to me
Yet you still escaped
But oh, they still say it
They say it like it's true
They say it for me and you
And I would tell them they're wrong
Because it's your home where I belong

Faitytale

Bewildered was I
To think that I could find
Love
How they write it in the books
If I see it, how does it look
Are the movies quite true?
Will my eyes meet before we're through
Will the sun shine when it's blue
Or will I avoid all salient clues
Shimmering
Or is it just a reflection
Like the moon has of the sun
Or the diamond in the rough
Grey clouds
All over my house
The raindrops cursing my vows
Maybe I was wretched
After all, it's all my fault
Should've broken the mirror
When I saw that smile
It wasn't worth all this while
The massacre
It passed my bones but left my heart all alone
Maybe I know why
Forlorn should it die

LOVE Poem

If love was a poem
I would write it for you
If Love Was a song
I would sing it for you
If love was a dance
I would learn every step for you
If Love was a promise
I will make it to you
But the Love I've known
Is the dark side of you

Undeserving Lover

He stands ahead of my door
Every morning
Holding a cigarette in his hand
Poisoning the air surrounding
Causing me to react
To shout, to talk
He looks at me with pleading eyes
Bleeding regret, apologies
But I ran out of forgiveness
So I close the doors
Hide behind them and grieve

Metro Spectacle

She lost him
In the dawn
Still thinking what her life has become

He couldn't catch the train
He couldn't be on time
Maybe both lost the love of their lives

Maybe if time was a little slow
In stealing memories and people away
She was sure she'd find a way

He doesn't know where he's gone
From where he may never come again
He kept blaming these lifeless hands

Her tears filled the eyes of the watcher
Leaving the hearts in evermore ache
A painful love to never have, to never do

Brown Eyes

I fell in love with her eyes
Those surreal brown eyes
Like forests on fire
When there's light inside
And as calm as autumn
When you need her by your side
I fell in love with her eyes
Those brown surreal eyes

Do Know me

Ask me where I belong
Where do my nights pass
And the morning waves
Ask me about my past
What hurts me the most
What people do I hate
Ask me my favorite colour
Even though you know it's blue
Ask me the reason for it
Ask me the reason why I am here
In the middle of nowhere
Stepping on every branch
Every root of this ocean
To find the answers myself
Which I want you to ask me
So I put my heart into it
And my soul in the acquisition

Homesick

You knew I was an orphic
Yet you chose to stay
I was homesick
So I ran away

Damn The Timing

And at the wrong time of life
Maybe I found the right person for me
But our impossibility kept me waiting
Till the right time came
But the time played such a game
He found the right one for him
But that person wasn't me
And that's how time played with me

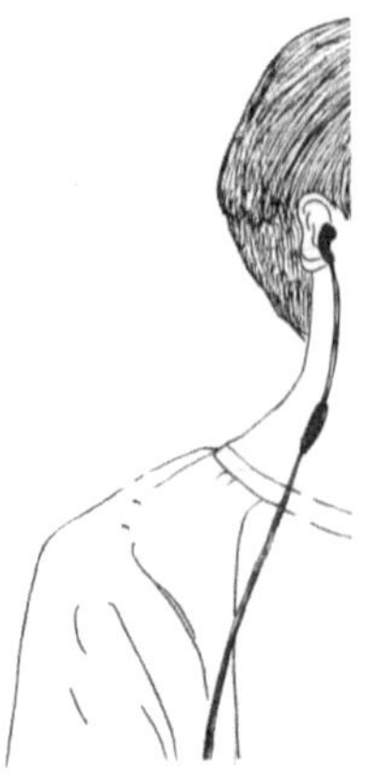

Dreamy Love

This love is better than movies
Perfect than all those book stories
It exists in the depths of the ocean
It shares the unseen emotions
Where is this love
The love which should be kept hidden
Is somewhere out there fighting the world
Somewhere inside keeping safe, it's worth

To Be a Criminal

Perhaps when I cried it wasn't a tear that I shed
But the fear of losing something greater
And when it touched my lips
I must've uttered the words that ruined my living
Because when I saw the world with my eyes
I saw all darkness and the hearts that I broke
So it must be true that when I cried
The universe must be smiling
And my soul must be in relief
To be separated from a criminal
And for as much as I remember
The only crime I commit
Was to say that I loved you

You were a monster

I knew I missed your scented white shirt
That wrapped around my body and made me whole
I knew I kissed your head
when we first met
Just to make you my own
I knew I left the house without locking the door
You slept all across the room
Knocking the floor
You crawled in filthy motions
On the carpet of my shore
Where I knew I left my heart
Open for you under the swore

Percfection

Not that I think of you
As perfection
But I presume it
How you think of me
As the perfectionist

Smokes And Ashes

Smokes and ashes called my name
They thought that I was your mistress
I wore a dress too short for my taste
So tight it could swing me away
I sang so loud, that my lungs filled with pain
Your ashtray empty, and for a long time it stayed
I lift my hand and those voices collide
It's just like waves and sand, close but never alive
You burned my skin with cigarettes you lit
I painted it with ink, that only you could kiss
I filled your drink with the blood I spilled
I know I could run but the line is thin
And these smokes and ashes could never win
The game they call it for love and sin

I'll put a mask On

Cuddled up in your sheets
You said you'll call me at three
It's been many hours since you left
And I feel this home suffocating
Left my glasses on as I sleep
I thought you'd take them off when you see
But it's been too long, it's been too late
Waiting here seems like misery
I stared at the ceiling for as long as I could
The green stares back and the black is cold
Our wedding photo hanging
Our smiles, so aligning yet so sore
I thought you said you loved me
Guess I was just hallucinating
Now each day I wait for the ending
But my heart said, 'Keep on pretending'

I won't Love

Love only knows hurting
It barely knows how to heal
I won't fall
I would never fall in love
Not being afraid of falling
But being afraid that
I'll lose all I have
All I get will be sadness and nothing else
Which will weigh on me for a lifetime

We would be

If we were not stars
We would be darkness
If we were not the ocean
We would be a lake
If we were not the chosen
We would be death

In Another Life

I've never known you enough
To call you mine
But I still think of you every time

I try to draw you out on paper
But I don't know your face
I don't know what I should chase

I thought that I could see you in my dreams
But I don't know if it's a good or bad one
If I should see you under the moon or the sun

I thought that maybe I could write about you
Because I imagine you in all forms
I could make you the sea or a storm

Instead of thinking I should've asked you
What you would like to be for me
But you desired to be a love without a guarantee

The Right One (I)

Love if you may
But let it be with your heart full
For a man who once loved
Neither forgets nor leaves till his last breath
And to be loved by a man
Who cherishes you so, praises and cares
Listens and understands
Is destiny to be found
Which you did not know was written

So love, if you may
But love the right man
For the wrong love will leave you empty
And with a void, no one could ever fill
He will come as a storm and take you in
Do not be loved by a man
Who steals your heart then throws it to dust
Misguiding and mistreating
A snake behind a mask, a terror behind the clouds

The Right One (II)

So love, if you may
But your love must be pure
As the lover you'll find deserves your world
May you be the one and he the only
For a man in love
Is in its whole glory, mighty and wondrous
Fulfilling and joyous
And for this match to be made
The stars aligned and the gods decide
That love if you may
But love one who'll pray

Luck

I was lucky to have you
But luckier to lose you

Her Lover and His Love

The yellow bird sings on the heaven's brim
And swings by the wind as it sees him
The hat and the stick and the wooden shoe
His cat traced it all to make them look new
The cigar lights with a lively strike
The fresh air exhaled by his bride
The white she wore, the black she threw on
So people would know, she's the loudest talk
Herself a desire, a running show of horses
She wouldn't for a penny, learn the dance courses
A rebel she was named, by the bird who sang
But heaven's heart closed with a bang
And she laughed the loudest on her man's face
As the medal she won, was for his race
So the cigar burnt the black gown and her in it
And the cat traced her ashes, tasting her unfit
So she would know who owns her life
It is no one but her lover's knife

Fault In Love

You don't tell me what to do anymore
Than I tell myself to get off the floor
The spirits crashing, knocking at my door
They ask for you, but you live here no more
You took your luggage, our life with you
I could just keep staring
In the shadow of that dried rose
Hanging by the wall, with the letters kept
On the side table by the door
They kill me, they scare me
They tell me I'm so lonely
I'm so lost so undeserving
I lost all my love, all my longings
I gave my blood, my tears, my heart
You packed it all and passed by the park
Where I told you I love you for the first time
You took me in your arms and we cried
But the spirits tell me I've been wronged
I've lived here all my life and never at all
I should've been the one you held in your hands
But it was our failed love that you buried there

SORROW

Never at All

I got your necklace around my neck
Your subtle kiss on my forehead
The apologies sound bitter now
But I have never been loved before
The flowers on my doorway
A letter that had your name
In it, I found some thorns
That cut my hands as I hold
Your excuses to tell why you weren't home
Last night when I cried myself to sleep
I told myself it was no war
But I have never been loved before
Sorry I stepped in your way
Sorry I called you by your name
Sorry I didn't get you coffee today
Sorry I acted out of my way
But I guess these sorries aren't enough
You stand proud as you hit me rough
But I got your roses and your texts
You say it was the last mistake
Then why do you come home to me
To watch me bleed on the floor
Perhaps I have never been loved at all

Night Tales

It wasn't the time
When he said it was
It wasn't all right
He said it wrong
All the night
He sings this song
His eyes in mine
The night was short
For my tears to dry
And my heart to be lost

Don't really find me

Find me where you can never go
To the places that are Hollow
Find me in the deepest of oceans
In the arms of the grass, and the beds of these thorny roses
Look for me where the sky is missing
All of your doubts are not believing
In what I say to you about me
You think of it as a fantasy
Yet you still find me
But at the wrong places every time
You find me in the day, but not in the night
You find me in your past
You look up to me as if I'm the last
Instead, I'm the beginning
Of every love story ever written and heard
I am the truth of fate, though it may sound absurd
But don't really find me
Don't find me at all
Because if I wanted to be found
I wouldn't be lost at all

Pessimist

Can't be complaining
For all the things I did
You showed me mercy
For all the blood I bled
Keep me your fantasy
No one to be seen as real
I'm nothing but insanity
A heart that can't feel

Disco Lights

Chaotic surrenders of open minds
Unlocked doorways of forgiven isle
Sins or sinners
Whichever arrives
Never reaches mournful crying
They climbed the states
Those disco lights
Broken chairs
Empty wines
Innocence fights day and night
In escapism from dreadful fright
The oceans dried
It lit souls on fire
Their hearts paralyzed
Pushing the end a little higher
But the curtains fell
They let it burn in hell
I carry these ashes of liars
Smoldered in sullied desires

You kept me in Doubt

There's an ache in my chest
For the person I can't forget
Widowed whites and cautious tales
They speak to me my fate
With the windows open
I see how you're dreaming
Through the cracked doors
We keep contemplating
You're still hiding under the covers
I keep the lights on so I can hover
Crooked smiles and bandaged fingers
They are writing my summer story
Waiting for the leaves to turn dark
So they could fall in glory
Fall in the morning
So when I see your face when years have passed
I will see all the marks, all the kisses scars
That I gave you but you hid them under my scarf
Wasn't it a gift, to keep the cold out
But I guess you use it to keep me in doubt
Was it necessary?
All the screaming at the cemetery
I thought I was buried
Till you called my name, were you imaginary?
That love was quite incendiary
But it was ours and will stay till our souls are weary

You Lied

I said I'm fine
And you believed it
I said I'd try
But you made me quit
I painted you like a garden
But you grew like thorns
You flew when you were done
And forgot me like I was never born

I painted you Grey

I think I painted your gardens grey
Left your hand astray
Broke all the codes walking on my own
Felt shallow when I left your home
Kept a secret lying on that bed
A Neverending Story Unread
Packed my moments in swollen hands
Tied a knot with broken strands
I think I painted your dreams empty
Not knowing that I was painting
Maybe I left your life blue
Forgetting mine was blue too

I am

The crushed memories of the darkest hour
The emotional prayers of smiling hearts
Sinful words of the loved souls
Are there in these shaking hands
Hope I don't fall apart, hope I don't break
I am all they have, am all for their sake

You went away

I wanted to tell you who I was
But you went away so early
I wanted to show you how I look in the dark
But you closed your eyes so soon
I wanted my voice to capture your soul
But you went deaf so quick
All I wanted was to tell you whom you loved
But you flew in those clouds
What you always wanted was to escape the crowd

Wait In The Dark

Wait until the end is here
Wait till the flowers cry and the shadows hide
Wait for me on the edge of the night
Where the lonely moon cries

Wait until you feel the time is here
At a time when the mountains will fade
All the raindrops will walk away
Wait for me there where we first prayed

But don't wait for me where you see hope
I'll be gone by that time for good
Just stay from where you can't elope
Stay and wait where everyone's heart broke

You'll find me there
Behind one of those corpses, I'll be hiding
To look at you with this death I'll be fighting
And when it is time our souls will be igniting.

Risk Taker

You seem so beautiful
But looks so sad
You seem to be regretful
Of a haunting past
You smell like after rain
But drowning in pain
You felt like a pillow
A pure soul, but Hollow
You seem to have found the answers
Of your past in today
Risking your future you save
As you drift it away

Human

I am a human
But today I am resentful
Being a human
A human who hates
Who is violent
Whose ego wins over
Who kills each other
I am ashamed
Being a human
Lacking humanity
And beginning wars
Which ends with nothing left
And for whom do we care
To stop all this for
Are we all not the same
Are we all not equal
As we come and will go
We were meant for equality
For justice and peace
We can live together
If we let each other breathe

Disregarded

Let me be hideous
Let me be gone
The crowd you search me in
Forgot that I was born

> Let me crawl on my bed
> Let me hide behind my books
> My Mates, they are fed
> Of my constantly distracted looks

Let me be a mistress
Let me be a slave
For pure hatred they find me
Knowing love isn't my fate

> Let me be a joke
> An anecdote in your journal?
> Your Polaroids will turn to smoke
> If you mark me in your circle

So let me be my demon
For this crowd thinks I was never alive
For each deed, I shall be the reason
I came here, maybe, to take my own life

Loving is Sin

Our souls spun together into bundles of mistakes and
forgiveness
Tangled along the veins with flowing demons inside of
them
Our fingers strangle and form a fist or to depart
Or shall we be mended in a way
That our sorrows form the lungs and our guilt form our
hearts
For this mind breaks and bleeds
On every fear and every darkness inside of me
Your eyes came looking for mine
But fell for what I call a sin
The sin I made, you made
Should I name it love
Or despair of fate
As a sin so impure and great
Should leave the earth hollow and the world lost in its state

Time Changed Me

At the pace of time
I forgot how you looked
I forgot to call out your name
I forgot to make you coffee
I forgot in wanting to believe
That you were a dream
Who came and went away
Just like childhood and old age
Just like wind and time
And just like the truth
I forgot you too

Do You Know Me? (I)

Why do you keep asking my name
When you are on the table with your hands on top of another
You read out loud the magazine cover
Drinking the juice out of the box
You laugh too loud while my soul suffers
You drew the painting that hangs on the wall
I find my face in it
It is flowers with a green vase
My shadow haunts the room
But you keep asking my name

You led me to the mountains in the car you bought
It smells kinda weird so I'd prefer if we walk
The clouds tug me closer
The ground seems awake
As I walk with the dandelions
You take your camera out
But then you ask my name

Do You Know Me? (II)

I ran out to the valleys where I saw a fire building
I was looking for the answers
To what I don't still keep finding
I cut, I bleed, I run, I scream
I do everything and anything but I get nothing
So I keep my face as I'm running
I run down, I cry out, I run from my mistake
I thought we could be saved
But yet you keep asking my name

I'd say it was Rose, I'd say it was Lily
But then tell me, dear, would the wounds start healing
All the years passed by and I still can't believe it
When I was your kingdom and you were there reigning
I gave you my throne and my crown with it
And I thought that we swore on the flame

That you won't forget my maim
So why do you ask my name
Why not just call me a shame
I vowed I'll take all the blame
So a curse now I have become
As I hang with my love as my pain

I'm not what you want, but what you need

All the crying ages
Left you wide open
All the dirty dishes
Wish someone could hold 'em

You keep breaking on your bed
Your papers on the ground
Don't do something you'll regret
Please keep that knife down

Oh, I know it's hard for you
Trust me I understand
It's not easy to get out of the blue
But I promise, I'll take your hand

And your home won't be a mess
You'll feel the warmth of sunlight
And I won't leave you again
If that means that you'll die

I would never make this promise
Never hug your filthy body
But I don't like the blaming
If the blaming is on me

And I would never touch your heart
As I would stop it from beating
But if that's what you want
I hope you're red when you're leaving

I was not Myself

I was a stranger in your bed you found on the street
I must've done something evil to be found like this
You gave me a roof over my head, food in my body
But you also gave me bruises, wounds that scare me
It's red all over again, but from where I first escaped
You remind me of a past, the one that I hate
After all, I was a stranger to even myself
Who didn't know her skin was someone else's wealth

Mirror

And now as we begin
Craving for revenge
Craving for war
Craving for our blood
We empty our hearts
We kill our humanity
For nothing but an end
Which will soon be near
And all we have to do is fear
'Cause we've shown who we are
Nothing more than an evildoer

Untamed

It's been 20 years
But the feeling is indifferent
Pocket lives and early fears
The only thing alive is this cigarette

2 seconds ago I think I saw you
Couldn't be hallucinating
I know you smiled too
The kind that made me fall for you

My eyes have been staring that way forever
I think they want to see you again
But if it was a dream, however
I think it was of when we were 10

I lost you a couple of times
Missed you here and there in the suffering
It never changes, this thing about time
But makes us change through learning

Although it seems I never learned
What it could mean to be this grown
To never have the heat again, and the thirst
To be someone, someone once unknown
Who still is a forgotten stone

Stone Cold

I hope you leave
When I close my eyes
Don't make me plead
I'm not sure what's right
I held onto you
As long as I could
But my love you grew
I just hoped I could too
And I won't be around
Even when you're gone
I buried my heart in the ground
It's better than carrying a rock
But I'll still wait for you
Breathing or in dust
While you walk through
Dead garden of my trust

Opposites I left (I)

And there I was
Hoping you might come back again
And things will be the same
Like a little candle, I lit when I was young
I remember the smell, it smelled like your hug
And I wish you could see it all
Hiding behind the curtains
Wishing you could be them
But you are your own person
And I was a slave of the heart
A peasant at your service
I never knew how they played this card
But guess they couldn't beat us
When all that lying on the floor
Was the ashes of the unopened memories
And I never had them all
Never re-lived your happy journeys
And when my heart still aches
It's like a game we used to play
I never won, and you never lost
'Cause of the rules we didn't obey

Opposites I left (II)

Now life had grown out on us
It grew and left us two corners of the river
Two parallels and opposites
Two broken glass with wine spills
Found you again now, under my bedsheet
Over my ceiling, between those pages
Behind those feelings
I hid it all, I hid all of you with parts of me
The parts that I could never be
As much as I loved you
I knew this release was what I need

Can't figure you out

A different meaning was believed
Of that story, I wrote about you
They thought you were the evildoer
But you were the harsh truth of me becoming

Been Wronged

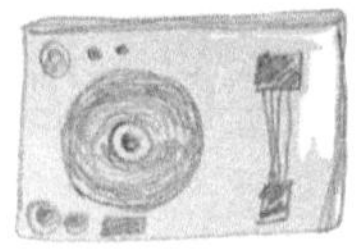

For once I thought you were the one
And that feeling lasted long
For once I thought we were meant to be
After you wrote that song
For once I thought I found my love
And I was sure where I belong
But now at once, I'm sure
That all this time I was so wrong

Never The One

Never loved and never seen
Nor a feeling for the skin
The wind was so wild, I hid
Under the surface of my ruins

My feet bled without a shoe
Hands bruised by sand homes
My ear burns to hear the truth
Of promises made of coal

I sit and listen, my heart wounded open
To the legends of your bravery
I bury deep my thoughts unspoken
Afraid of your forged victory

And I know I could never be, never could
The love and the mystery you wished
So I sit and listen over the firewood
The tales of the knight I never kissed

I Hate it (I)

I hate it when you say 'you're mine'
I don't think I even relate to you
I haven't gotten the same eyes
Or the same person we write to

I hate it when you call me 'love'
That word is as absurd as it becomes
I've never seen it, heard it, felt it
But I guess I'll take it if someone does

I hate it when you say 'how's your day'
I don't share with anyone, I barely care
But you seem to do a lot
A lot that I only hoped for and never dare

I hate it when you look me in the eyes
Are they telling you a story or a joke
If it's interesting write it on the side
I'll read it when I'm with you and bored

I Hate it (II)

I hate it that I hate it the most
The phrase 'I love you' like it's true
This thing between us is the worst
Something like a spoiled painting I threw
And it would deteriorate as I knew
'Cause a life with you, is where I withdrew

Who Are You?

Is it me
Or whom I used to be
Who makes you, you
Who you're supposed to be

We Separate (I)

When did we put those walls?
Outside our houses
Inside our homes

I see them everywhere now.
It's like that's all that we built
Obnoxious and unpleasant

I feel those walls often
When people fight
And break the ties
When the darkness rises
And scares us all

Somewhere outside the walls
There seems to be a day-rising
But inside I feel the grief in smiling

We Separate (II)

Maybe it's not their fault
Nor even of those who built it
We all do things to secure us
Maybe walls are there to protect us

But sometimes I wonder
If there were no bricks and no hands
To build something so menacing
Would there be any darkness
Down the roads, in the halls
Would there be any dejection
In people's homes, in their hearts

So I need to know when and who
But most of all why
Because the walls I see
Are we in human life

You're BLUE

I can't hate myself when I'm with you
Can't stop dreaming out of the blue
You fill me up with definitions and reasons
You fill me up with choices to believe In
But I could not love you as I loved myself
I could be swearing about all the threats
Lying on the floor
Painting all the blue
On me and you
I could lie and laugh
I could live and die
Pretending to be me
When it's just a lost dream
I could fight my battles drowning in the sea
Looking at the sky and finding you with a belief
How can you be so pure and selfless
And your love be so true and not so blue
And how can I be still wondering
Of all the sins I made, things I said
The rights I did wrong, the lives I killed
I could cut my vein for every tear because of me
I could turn the page and burn every story of me
But would that make me the monster I run from
The evil that causes me pain
The fear that makes me run to the blue
I'm not ever returning to you

What should I do?

Should my tears have your name?
Should I tell them who to blame?
I guess they missed their early train
Too late to reach, too fast I drained

I said I won't cry
over a boy I just liked
Isn't that so stupid, so lame?
You didn't even know my name

So now I'm hiding from my family
My friends think I'm fine because I'm smiling
But I'm just used to it all
The rejections on the call

And now there's an ache in my chest
Shouldn't I have butterflies instead?
Was I just another girl you had?
To let down, to let go mad

To let her sit on her couch
And listen on repeat, songs so sad
Or was it really my fault?
To want someone I wasn't supposed to want?

Existence

How did I go from flying like a bird to a drowning boat
How did I step on caskets while reading notes
I remember being in that old house near the stream
But the next moment I was in a haunting dream

DEATH

Two Graves

'Cause even when we fade
I hope I'm still awake
To see the colors we paint
On the coffins which we made.

I wanted to run (I)

Just some words I was writing
Under the shade of the sun
When I saw someone smiling
Behind the woods, so I run
I ran from a smile
I ran a couple of miles
I paused to catch my breath
Slid onto the grass and gasp
As I stretched through the length
I heard a loud tap
So I ran
I ran again, but now in the dark
I ran again, away from the park
This time I stood still, as
The moon called it midnight
I thought of what a day I had
Until I turn and again see that smile
I didn't run
I couldn't run
The smile had a face this time
A face so alluring to run away from
Those eyes were looking into mine
I tried to feel it, but I turned numb

I wanted to run (II)

I wanted to run
I wish I could run
He held me in his arms
He carried me on his back
I fainted against his cards
After it all my thoughts were black
And I felt like souls on a stack

Expectations

For what seems real to me
Keeps fading like a memory
As much as I try to hold on
It keeps getting a hold of me

The waves I thought were calm
Are storming inside my mind
I walked and walked and walked
Till the day burned blind

I was supposed to be Awake
To be what everyone else wanted me to be
I guess I kept disappointing
In my greed to be me

But as long as I hold this promise
That I'll come back to where I belong
I'll leave every heaven, every door
To match every piece I kept wrong

Too Lost

I was there
But still couldn't feel it
I thought it was rare
Then those lies reveal it
I saw the lights coming out
But couldn't let go of the dark
I guess I was too lost to shout
So I left on those souls a mark

Incomplete

Not a word left so wise
Which I could scream while looking into your eyes
Not even a drop of a tear
That would always fall when you were near
Not a single night of sleep
Since I fell into your words so deep
It's only been a thread
From which I keep myself hanging
So I do not fall again
For wishing for what's worth having

I Can Free Them

I think of myself
When I was lying there
When the night was weeping
And the stars were screaming
The moon closed his eyes
And let clouds pleading
To the sun to never come up
They may never burn
They may never turn
Their faces around
From the dark to the light
They must cross the wind
They must lie deceased
They must call my name
I know the sense of maiming
I think I can help them escape
After I free myself from this cave

Effectful

The unheard voices
They shout to me at night
The silent dreams
Let people wipe their eyes
I don't know what needs to be seen
As what is ever seen is destroyed
But as long as this night is awake
It won't let me feel paranoid
For the living and the dead
The light and the dark
Both have an impact on me
And left me with eternal marks

Weird (I)

It's weird how I like grief so much
It's weird how I think things take a turn and that they have
to go through a bad phase
It's weird when I say that I like your voice, I like your eyes
when they're just so normal
It's weird when I want you to brace, but I just hold your
hand and say goodbye
Because I know it's weird for me to ask you to stay, so I let
you go
And it's weird how I want to write about all that pain that
came to me, all the pain that you gave me
All the sadness and the tears, all the pain and all the sorrow
The sorrow which comes to me every night and whispers in
my ears
It reminds me of you, my dear
My pillow says to me now, that I don't like how weirdly
you're holding me the whole night
My kitchen doesn't like the weird taste I adapted and how I
do not keep it clean anymore
It's weird how my curtains are never drawn now like the sun
might be ashamed to see me, or I might burn when seen
It's weird when I think all of this is weirdly me and all of me
is weirdly true

Weird (II)

It's weird why I am writing about it in the dark sitting on
my bed in a weird position that I might break my bones in
But my mind is also in a weird state, and so is my heart
So I let it stay like this
Because I know it's weird to be dreaming about it, and
cursing the reality in which I'm drowning
It's weird that I am still writing

Why?

I'll let your oceans free
Once you let me breathe
I'll let you feel the need
Once I know what I feel
I'll tell you all the secrets
Of the night, and the weakness
On the day, when the sun
Answers my questions
Why do I even need to breathe
Why do I have to sleep
Why do I need to cry
Why can I not fly
Why do all my doubts
All my worries shout
Why am I left unanswered
Why am I still in a meander

Timeline

And I could not say
Neither mention it
What was the thing
Which was hurting me
Was it the past
Or the future I expect
Or is it the present
Which seems so wrecked

Beliefs of Mine

But I should go
And I must go
I must leave these valleys
And go ahead of these forests
I should crave the paths
With my own fingers on the ground
I must deceive my beliefs
Even though I know I don't have any
But I do have hope
Hope like having a spark in the dark
Having a house on the sand
Keeping my feet on the oceans
And sleeping on the clouds
I know I might be wrong
But I might not be so wrong

Death Whispered

When death talked to me
It talked so calmly
It felt so warm
It showed no signs of sadness
No stages of vain
It showed escaping
With no bitterness of pain
What a fool I was
To trust all of that
To trust my own death
Which took me away
From everything I had
From everyone who was sad
As it took me away
Just because I didn't want to stay

Life or Death

Make death be drowning in vain when it takes me
To be crying tears of regret when it holds me
Make it known that the fault lies in the hands of those
whom it left alive
The fault lies in those who won't let people like me survive
And what about the life they asked me
What should I say about such a thing which is meant to be
holy but is as evil as the world?
I would say death is still better than life
At least it makes us stop feeling the cruel ice

Fool for Eyes

How well do you know the impact
Of the words you say out loud
Is still a mystery to me
To find blue out of the clouds
But you carry it so well
Like if perfection was real
And I read what your eyes tell
So words seem hard to appeal

No Apathy

To know what's your last wish
I climbed your walls barefoot
To save you from the demons
I burned the kingdoms they put
I died in agony for you
While you were still unknown
That the one who saved you
Was a soul in me

I said Goodbye

I held my wreath in my hands until I was told that I didn't
deserve any
I was supposed to be leaving in secrecy
But the world sent me like an occasion
Which I was not expecting any time in this life to happen
But as soon as it did
I knew where I would disappear to

Disappearing Act

And before I knew
You were gone
In the depths of the sea
Through the dawn

And before I see
The tears you hide
You embraced the sea
With your fond smile

I'll go to Hell

I ate my own heart
For this hunger is endless
And this world cannot understand
Why my breathing is restless

As I stole my own soul
It opened the doorway
And to hell I'll go
Without calling your name

They Ask me to Sleep (I)

I keep soaking in the words I read
They tell me I need to sleep

I write at midnight when you crawl out of your bed
Coffee or tea, or Just warm water
Which is it that you'll drink
I imagine your steps and I write my words
Your feet mark my sentence and your shadow is my page
Yet again your eyes tell me I need to sleep

I don't dream, I can never do
I say I'm afraid of being at odds
You open the fridge and you join the dots
You make me weep as you mind your thoughts
I can see and I can read
Your thoughts as though they're in me
It kills me to tell, what everyone keeps telling me
I wonder why they all think I need to sleep

They Ask me to Sleep (II)

I'm awake when I die and I scream when I'm alive
I smile seldom and I grieve as I breathe
I've been called names
I've been called names
I make them my identity, I let them take my place
So when another shadow another word or another
thought comes my way
I will run and I will die
And on my grave, they'll write
'She never felt too deep, at least she's finally asleep'

Smudged Memories

It rained all through my drive
As I was leaving your town
I asked you if you cared enough
But you only looked down
I read your guilty eyes
The brown and the red in them
It talked to me when you didn't
As I asked the same again
I remember when we were kids
You used to write me letters
Those funny words and the smudged ink
The memory now gives me terror

Pretty Woman

You leave your lights on when you sleep at night
You clench your teeth and you hold onto the sheets as you try
To let go of the dreams that haunt you at midnight
So you hid behind the bed and hope it all flies

The curtains open but you don't look outside
You keep your eyes closed till they tell you it's time
You write on the wall how you thought you'd die
But the ink didn't fall, it stayed inside

The knock on the door, you say that you're fine
The clock on the wall, you can't tell what's the time
As you lay there on your hopes that dried
You forgot how much and for whom you cried

Now all that is left are the knots untied
With which you tied yourself day and night
But watch the roads as a runaway bride
Who knew that all in her life was just a lie

A Statue

For a long time
I stayed where I was
My feet frozen to the ground
Time stopped in my hands
The air shallow and my breathing fast
The sky crumbled and fell on me
But I didn't move an inch
For how long I could see
I saw the destruction from where I stood
I saw mirrors destroy both inner and outer selves
I saw hands ruining each other's body
I saw eyes hunting for survival
I saw mouths whispering sins to each other
I stayed there and I witnessed it all
As my own body still and my soul sour
I saw them running toward me and I gasped
I stay united by my front and I stay quiet
I got ruined and I got annihilated
I didn't scream, I didn't run, I didn't protest
I stay there and watch them havoc
The entirety of them and every piece of mine
Their Wipeout called out for me in the end
And then I stood up from my pedestal
And raze everything to thin air

I still see you

It never occurred to me
That life is, what it could be
An ancient history
Shared by a torn painting
The faded colors and the empty faces
They remind me of what I lost
My heart at haunted places
From when for long I was lost
In the woods, in the rain
Shattered dress, wounded ankles
Untouched ache with unknown pain
Until I found the spark in unlit candles
And I walked through the hallway
Holding on to dear life and the painting
Till I heard the tyres screech on the highway
Where I lost you as you were fainting
In my arms, lies a lifeless body
The painting and the candles
Told me it was a repetition of history
Of decades ago, death by the furnace

No More Flowers

No more flowers on my doorway, please
No more letters of that cold breeze
The light you kept on
Could be turned off again
Those candles of the dawn
Will blow off by the rain
Is it your heart or your guilt
That you keep coming to my home
The home which we both built
But where I lived alone
I hope I could tell you I quit
The life I lived in dreams
So stop trying to admit
That it wasn't as it seemed
So no more flowers on my doorway, please
No more water on the dead trees

Deal-Breaker

To be given is a heart of gold
Someone who takes is a priest
Never above, never throned
Someone who did is a thief
This book shines regardless of being old
It says don't let go of your peace
But the guilty never spoke
As peace remained on its feet
So a song was written, or so I was told
Never sung, never said with a beat
No note of it was ever heard
But I see the fate, the destiny unfold
As someone great and elite,
Too cold
Left me hanging on repeat
As the thief who was never too bold
Hid all this time, underneath

I'd die first

I had to lose myself to keep up with the life I dreamt of
It was fast-paced so my speed had to go up
Saw the buildings and the roads with tricks on two feet
Mistook it as a lifestyle that I could live, guess they tricked
me
I fired up, I got tired, and I dreamt of it once, guess I got
caught up
In the reflection they show but never see themselves
In the play they carry but forget to give them a character
They look for something in an object someone could give
'em
The something that needs to be defined, that only they
could have them
I hear the tyres screech, the mothers scream, and the sisters
dream
All on the floor of the red roads I was once walking on
Do I get to see what this turtle had dreamt of
I went to his mother, looked into her doleful eyes and
asked
Did your son live his life the way he wanted to?
Was he happy and did he smile when he reached home to
you?
She looked at me, unfathomable her eyes cried, but with a
smile, she tried
'If only I could ever know, I'd be the one who'd first go'

Midnight Called

I thought it was rain
But it's just the wind playing with the trees
I woke up to see it, to feel it
But the darkness held me as it pleased
I stepped out of my bed
The door was locked, and my hands frozen
I had a thought I would regret
But breaking it open was what I wanted
I thought it was raindrops
But turned out they were just tears
I left my state for nothing
And it caught hold of my fear
I still run for the clouds
Hope they can see through me
Because I could never say it out loud
But I needed that breeze
To take me away
To find me a home
With no clue from where I came
I sit under that tree, alone, in vague hope

Were you a Dream?

Your bands wrap the armour
Letting the blood from spilling
Your strength shields my corner
But I no longer believe in it

You crawled into my skin
Protecting me from within
And I knew I could never pay
Back, the love you gave me

And every time I go back
You're not there, not even here
And every time I come to look for you
They say you were just in the air

A Person

A mind not cease to think
A heart not stopped from beating
A soul reminded to care
A hand to give and bear
An eye to save the tear
A foot to touch the ceiling
A rose to be kept on the desk
A flame on the letter I held

A lantern till my way home
A home not emptied by loneliness
A home not abandoned by grief
A blink to change it all
A ring to break it all
A promise to be mine
Another to be not here at all

Should've Kissed The Tree

I kiss the dying leaf
For it has fallen too deep
Has been crushed by many feet
Won't be saved if I leave

I kiss the dying leaf
I give it a soft touch of me
A touch to help it breathe
I wish a helpless could be seen

I kiss the dying leaf
For it deserves to live
It deserves to be flying free
I'd give it a beautiful dream

I kiss the dying leaf
As something too is dying inside me
Which can't be saved by poetry
Can't be saved by a kiss on the cheek

I'm Not You

Do not fill my cup too
As you fill yours with sorrow
Mine should remain empty until
I find my boulevard to follow

Short Story

Walk forever with me
But never name us
Give me all you want to
But never expect in return
Tame me if you want
But never blame for your bad
Make me the villain so
But don't dare to ask the reason

They Had Me

The shadows were all I had
The moon was what I wanted
To get it I lost my shadow
I now trust it was my only destiny

History Forever

That breeze was cold enough
To chill my bones
The sky was dark enough
To fear my soul
The lightning was adequate
To shiver up my whole body
Those storms were in abundance
To cry my heart out again
The light was never seen after that
Horrible anecdote you wrote
Those heavenly bodies above that dark sky
Were dead forever
This is the history going to repeat
After you steal my heart again

We've Drifted Apart

Our roads have disengaged
Our destinations are now far away
No one knows where you are nor me
Our helplessness increased swiftly
I wanted that sky but you fell in love with the ground
The conversations which were unsaid
Are still incomplete
Our lips don't utter a word now seeing each other
And our eyes have also gone quiet
You faded away like those clouds
And I still silently stare at that sight

Darkness

I will never be the sunlight
That shines upon you
I will never be the candle
That you keep in your room
I will never be the rhyme
That you keep humming on
I will never be the rain
That falls upon you
I will never be the bird
That sings every morning on your window
Because I am the darkness
That you keep hidden within yourself

Dark Knight

If I were afraid of this darkness
I would keep my candles along
But I walked with my eyes closed
In these forests where I don't belong
My courage sat beside me
When I talked to the crows
My hands didn't shake for the first time
When I made a tiara from the rose
My heavy eyes glimmered
Under the moonlight
My sad smile said it all
That I now won this fight

What's on your grave?

Do they call you by your name
Do they know that you even have one
A rather beautiful maim
Engraved with a blame

Just take your shame with you
Take your fame with you
They don't know your home
Take your mate with you

I carried your weight
Of sorrow and pride
All these years await
And you still never cried

Do they call you by your name
Do they even know you that well
To sit along and give a hand
To feel you under the shell
To shed a tear on your farewell

Insane

Half drunk, half sane
Spiral heart, mind in vain
Spilling out my child's play
To make and break and fit right
It's high on the line, line

Second page, second side
Tape on my mouth, words in and out
Cross it wrong, dark rhyme
To wish and pray and curse fine
It's black and it's red wine, wine

But I've been under it for long enough
Yes I've been under it all my life
So crush it down, on my feet
Make it bleed and plead, so sweet
Let go of my hand, let it free
And let it swing around
Choking my heart out
These monster growled
To end it right here, right now

Ending It Right

But when the time ends
I'll begin to write 'you'
Cause when one story ends
I crave for the new
Settle for the show
It'll leave you latent
The night will never grow old
Still don't try to be patient
I'll call it the ending of my existence
Once and for all
The battle of my persistence

If I Would

But if I could never love like this
I would never love at all
If I could never breathe in the mist
I wouldn't be born from the dawn
If I would be living in a dream
I would be living with a crown
If I would be singing a song
I wouldn't sing it from my mouth
If I was crying under my blanket
Were those my tears or my lifelessness
If I was driving blindly
Was I driving over to you
If I would be captivating me
I would be behind the glasses
If I would be lying to you
I wouldn't ever say the truth
But if I could never live this life
I would be dying in heaven

A Regular Night (I)

Couldn't write so I stared at the ceiling the entire night
Hoping words might fly through and settle in my mind
Wishing that the air would make me feel better
My bed kept getting warmer where I was awake
And as cold as the heart of a lover beside me
I touched it gently
The bed, my thoughts, the air, the hopes

Couldn't think straight so I sat on the side of the mattress
I was about to fall, but I was too afraid to shatter on the
floor
So I held onto the wall beside me like I held onto the sea
I was out of breath, I didn't know how to survive in the
ocean
My lungs filled with water and wanting to escape it
While the entire world needed what I hated
I stopped trying, kicking my feet, moving my hands around
I touched the ground, the deep sea of my mind, of my life
It was as dark as the deep end, as the high above
As quiet and still as a midnight, as a dead life

A Regular Night (II)

Couldn't breathe so I left my room, left my home
Didn't realize leaving my soul would hurt this time
My feet felt stones and blood and pain
My eyes looked for the heaven's gate
In front of me all these eyes could see, was darkness as far as
it could reach
Behind me was home
The soul I left behind
But when I stopped, it all burned down
And I knew then, running would be the death of me
And stopping was already a mire

I don't want to write

Whom do I write for
I have no friend so dear to write her a letter
Not the family that could understand the words I feel
Not a lover who makes me complete
I got no doll, which held me when I was a kid
No favourite artist whose music makes me weep
I have no desire to be known by somebody
No wishes, no hopes to name it holy
If I write then what do I write for
They already wrote for the trees, about the desire
For the love and the hate, the cold and fire
They already wrote for yesterday and the future they want
For their eternal and the ones they lost
Why do I write in the first place
If the dead can't read it and the soulmate is not found yet
If the trees only got ears and fire and cold got no plea
But if I still write
Who and what do I write about
If I write about the green and the waves, then I am Frost
If I write about dreams and passion, then I am Byron
If I write lust, if I write love, then Kafka should I be called
If I write about myself and the sea, then I am just another poet
And if I write about 'us', oh then I think
I'll either be the greatest or the prosaic
To be writing about the epic, love

POSTSCRIPT

After spending days of reading, editing, titling and designing my very first poetry book, we've come to the end of it.

But it is not the end of the series. The preparation for the next part is already on par.

This book has made me realise that all the mishaps and wrong things can also lead to something fruitful. After feeling like a failure more than a dozen times, this book has sparked a ray of hope in me.

This book has shown me that I can achieve my dreams too.

If you enjoyed reading, do share your feedback or any helpful suggestion on my email - lakshitavwrites@gmail.com.

Until Next Time.